Chronic Conundrums

A Century of Reflection

{1984 – 2004}

JD Magruder

Published by: 4D Productions
               PO Box 5659
               Aiken, SC 29804

Published in arrangement with Lulu Press (www.lulu.com).

Original publication date: April 1, 2005

First Edition

ISBN   1-4116-3034-3

Made In The U.S.A.

Dedication

This book is dedicated to my family, my lovers, my friends and my enemies. To everyone who had an impact on my life, both good and bad, I could not have written the works herein without you. To my family, friends, and lovers: Godspeed, good luck and long life! To my enemies: May you all suffer eternal in whatever hell spawned you.

A special dedication to Ms. Jeannette Robinson, educator extraordinaire. More than just an English teacher, she inspired and motivated and enlightened. She is the primary reason I would even consider publishing a book of this nature.

Introduction

Poetry is many things to many people. Personally, I consider it to be one of the highest forms of literature, as well as the most freely expressed. Like love or rock 'n' roll, poetry cannot be "defined" in terms of boundaries and restrictions. Poetry is, at times, the most passionate expressions of thoughts or ideas possible.

Lyrical poetry, as I understand it, is just that…poetry meant to be spoken or sung, possibly with a musical accompaniment; such as with the minstrels of the Middle Ages or a modern-day rock band. In short, lyrical poems are song lyrics without the music; unless one happens to be lucky enough to hear the author perform the poem live. The majority of my poems are intended to be lyrical. In fact, some of them originally started out as song lyrics but were never set to music.

The poems in this book are arranged fairly chronologically but not completely so. As I wrote them, the inspirations often came in waves and, as such, the poems did as well. For the most part, I have always kept them in that order. The exceptions being that some poems just have their particular sequence and are placed where I like them best. For example, the poem *Bachelorhood Unbridled* always begins this collection; and the poem named *Are You Receiving Me?* always ends it.

As for my style, I consider this collection to be "blue jean poetry." That is how the majority of them were written, in blue jeans; and probably with a drink in hand and music playing in the background. They are casual works, defined only by the inspiration behind them at the times they were written. The subjects within range from love to hate, from passion to depression, and from reflection to wonder.

I prefer to work with rhyme and meter; and often confine my poems to concise, efficient works; rather than filling page after page with redundant detail. Sometimes, in my opinion, a nice short and clear little rhyme can have just as much impact as a longer poem.

I have already heard many of the criticisms of my work: not enough descriptive detail, use of cliché terminology, etc., etc. I have listened to these criticisms and weighed them for myself over time. In some cases, I have made changes; whereas with others, I did not. Some poems have been edited over and over, while others remain unchanged from their original handwritten versions. For myself, poetry is not something that "should be" this or "should not be" that. My poetry is personal, it drips with life, and it says something to someone…mainly me; and hopefully to you as well.

Finally, I do not personally consider myself to be a "great poet." I simply write poems…whether good or bad will be your opinion after you read them. I have carried some of these poems around with me for the last 20 years, as both my reflections of the past and armor for the future. I am publishing them now as a result of the prodding of others who I've shared my work with; as well as in fulfilling a promise to myself to one day do so.

I hope in the course of reading these poems that you get something out of them for yourself. If you do not enjoy them, at least understand what it is you don't like about them; and take it upon yourself to write something better!

JD Magruder

Contents:

Chronic Conundrums

chron-ic *adj* [fr. Gk *chronikos* of time, fr. Gk *chronos*] (1601)
1: marked by a long duration or frequent occurrence; **2:**
always present or encountered; *esp:* constantly vexing,
weakening or troubling.

co-nun-drum *n* [origin unknown] (1645) **1:** a riddle whose
answer is or involves a pun; **2 a:** a question or problem having
only a conjectural answer; **b:** an intricate and difficult
problem. [*syn:* see MYSTERY]

Bachelorhood Unbridled

To exist using the enjoyment of women
As the sole purpose towards any uncertain goal,
Is to rule out all other possibilities
And to revolve around other people's realities,
To achieve an end result subsequently
Compatible to that of happiness.

Quarters

Dancing on crystal,
A silver circle spun 'round;
And, having done so,
Leaped lopsided down.

A cheer arose,
From the crowd all around;
"The shooter must drink!"
To the rules he was bound.

The drinker drank,
And, as luck he found,
He obeyed all the rules,
Before hitting the ground.

A cheer again,
From the crowd all around;
Laughing and pointing,
At the sight and the sound.

"The chair is open!"
The winner looked 'round;
But not a peep was heard
From the crowd all around.

"Then I win again!"
Was the only slurred sound
As the winner stood up
And promptly was downed.

A final cheer,
From the crowd all around;
The party re-fueled,
By the sight and the sound.

Drowning

Dark, cloudy,
Murky shapes;
Awareness!
Water everywhere!
Surrounding, threatening,
Embracing body and mind.

Hope!
A vague light!
Swimming, hoping,
knowing,
You can do it.

Suddenly!
Lungs are tight,
Burning,
Over-filled with air,
Threatening to burst.

Fear!
You feel your sweat,
Even in the water's wet,
Slippery grip.

Swimming!
Lungs straining,
Muscles aching,
Brain numbing.

Surface!
Bursting upwards,
Like a jolted fish;
Mouth open,
Head shaking,
Devouring the air.

Looking!
Straining to see
Anything;
Hope fleeting,
Bobbing,
Floating,
Waiting.

Color Vision

"Life is a point of view!"
Echoed in my head;
In a schizophrenic dream,
Seething purple and red.

"The purpose of Life is
To eventually die;
And the workings of Man
Are prophesied lies."

"Not true," said The Other,
On a mushroom he sat,
"How do you know if
You know where it's at?"

"I agree," I added,
Floating by on a cloud;
Listening in earnest
As they debated aloud.

"I have seen all there is
And to me it is so,"
Said Cain the Immortal
With a fiery glow.

And in the next instant,
On the cloud that I stood,
I found to my surprise
It was made out of wood.

I started to sweat
And my mind to slip,
Then remembered
I was on a chemical trip.

I flew to The Other,
Called over to Cain;
The three of us fused and
I was whole once again.

13

Ant Bites

A blade!
A blade!

I need a razor!
Because my arm
Burns like a laser!

Fire!

The little white peaks
Are tensing my cheeks
As I touch the swollen flesh.

Let me cut it!

Cut it right off if I have to,
To stop this pain;
Oh, it drains me.

I can't think straight,
Can't hardly wait,
Hand me the blade!

….Ahh!

That feels good!
So good!
Slice it up!

Let the fuzzy blood
Run free!
Free, right out of me!

Window

On my wall I have a window,
Yet more a wonder than a window be;
For in the morn, when the sun strikes,
I am called, drawn, as if pulled
By strings to the simple pane.

As I open the window, I see her,
Draped in all her glory;
Dumbstruck, I smile,
No words do I utter
To disturb the tranquil scene.

Nature has outdone herself
This fine morning;
And I am pleased beyond earthly measure.
Then, to my displeasure,
A knock upon the door.

Loud and depressing as funeral bells;
A disturbance that tears me away
From my love, her vivid scene
Imprinted firmly in my heart.

A parting glance…

Awakening

It can be seen in the sunsets,
In print and on TV;
A vast awareness growing,
Such a sight to see.

And the eyes of Posterity open…

It can be heard on the airwaves,
With people asking "Why?"
And youth, precious youth,
Continuing to try.

And the eyes of Posterity widen…

It may take too long,
A lonely eon or two;
But I keep pen in hand
To try to help the world too.

And Posterity is awake!

Bewildered

Why is it one can
See more clearly
When times are darkest?

And when can my friends
Stop poisoning themselves
To prove society's wrongs?

And when will starving children
Be a fairy-tale of the past,
A moral to be practiced and preached?

Please tell me why
The younger ones must die
To prove the mistakes of the old?

And just how long
Must this torment go on
Until we live in true peace at last?

What?!?

What?!?
What do you want?
Do you need something from me?

What?!?
What do you want?
Is it not enough to be free?

Is this a game,
You play with my mind?
I just do not understand
What you hope to find!

Do you think, perhaps,
That I'll manage to try
To explain Life to you
While I'm asking you "why?"

What?!?
What do you want?
Do you need something from me?
You refuse to leave me be!

Why Do All The Drummers Die?

Sometimes, while I'm in bed,
Strange thoughts run through my head;
Like why I have to ask "Why?"
And why do all the drummers die?

Then, as always, it comes to mind,
A truth so great is hard to find;
And so bakes the fruit of the pie
But why do all the drummers die?

Still I climb the Stairway
And still I hear the Who;
I wonder why the drummers die
And ultimately, so must you.

Even now, as I lie in bed,
Spinning images turning red;
I daydream when I see the sky
And wonder why the drummers die.

How On Earth

How on Earth
Are we expected to know,
The fruits that result
From the seeds that we sow?

And how on Earth
Can we decide and act
And properly manage
Relations with tact?

And what on Earth
Are we expected to do,
When we find that the facts
Are no longer true?

And how in the name
Of everything right,
Can I be true to myself
And still sleep at night?

Screaming at the Sky

Jesus Christ,
Where am I?
Halfway between
Hell and Sky?
I try so hard
Just to get by!
Where the hell
Does time fly…
Anyway?

Ode To Elena

She arrived before the dawn,
She danced her dance
And sang her song;
And put her vengeful visage on.

Like a twirling prima she spun,
As she danced her dance
And sang her song;
Her vengeful visage baring down.

Half a million people fled with fear,
As she danced her dance
And sang her song;
Her vengeful visage glaring down.

Some celebrated her sojourn,
As she danced her dance
And sang her song;
Her vengeful visage staring down.

For three days she did not move,
As she danced her dance
And sang her song;
Her vengeful visage wearing down.

The people grew careless waiting,
As she danced her dance
And sang her song;
Her vengeful visage turned to frown.

Her nose turned up, she turned to leave,
As she danced her dance
And sang her song;
Her vengeful visage nearly gone.

The people heaved a great sigh,
As she danced her dance
And sang her song;
She tossed her vengeful visage down.

A careless few shook their fists
As she danced away;
But those who knew
Bent their knees for a grateful pray.

It Seems I Dream

To writ,
To have writ;
This and more
To be remembered for.
Ahh! Such a thought!

But no, not even
In my wildest,
Flamboyant
Fantasies of the deep
Unconscious.

To wit,
To have wit;
And still more,
For four or five
Still left to drive
My memory.

God willing,
Lest the public
Taunt my name
Towards some infinitely
Finite degree of recognition.

King's Day

Today is King's Day;
Yet, *The King*'s day?
I should think not;
Yet, a great man indeed.

A blind man sees;
Yet, does he lead?
I should hope not;
But a great man, indeed.

Bleak Outlook

What good is sunshine,
With nothing to shine upon?

I can only hope and pray
My flower does not die,
Robbed of her happiness,
With no sun in her sky.

And what of the sun itself?

Deprived of purpose,
Forced into darkness,
With nothing to care for;
With no place to shine?

What good is sunshine,
With nothing to shine upon?

Reassurance

Everyday I work, I earn;
Everyday I live, I learn
That there is more to learn
Than what I know.

Every time I try to write
I get a dreadful fright
That the words won't rhyme;
The meaning is unclear.

It is hard to care about everything
And not be able to dance or sing;
For depression is a lonely thing.

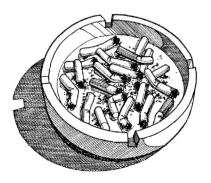

Blood Oaths

Don't you know
That my Father,
When I was young,
Told me not to bother
With the iron lung?

Can't you see
That even he
Could not be alive,
If wires and buttons
He needed to survive?

I have to do it;
I have to pull the plug;
No matter what crime
Or charge made to me,
I'll do it out of Love.

Youth in Asia,
Dying in the streets;
Euthanasia,
Letting go the weak;
Don't let it phase ya',
It's relief they seek.

Johnny

Hello!
My name is Johnny
And though
You may think it funny,
I have 6 billion people
In my house.

They all live in groups,
Such patriotic troops;
Each afraid the others
Will discover…

That really,
We're all the same,
There's no point to the game,
And no one's going to win.

Jerri

You have arrived, I contrive;
For your knock is like music
On my otherwise hollow door.

As you enter, your perfume
Permeates my brain to the point
Of an insane burst of rhymes
And meaningless phrases.

Your dark sparkling eyes
Pierce the room with a warm,
Romantic glow, and
Cast away my gloom
And depression alike;
Placing laughter in their stead.

To feel, to touch
Your countenance
With absorbing eyes,
Puts me in a strangely
Sad feeling of contentment;
As I dread to see you leave.

Hot Air

My Love is a balloon,
Which constantly floats
Over a field of roses;
Your beauty and your splendor.

As you draw nearer and closer,
The fire of your beauty
Heats the air of passion inside,
Expanding the balloon to bursting.

Desire swelling, straining
And stretching the skin,
Threatening to split or tear
From the growing pressure.

The balloon flies me over
Your splendid beauty, roses
Look up at me from below;
Smiling and glowing red.

Almost touching your petals,
Floating nearer and closer,
Love and pride alike
Straining to reach you.

Finally, contact!
Reaching you and your touch;
My love softly lands in your field,
Parting the flowers, gentle pressure.

You sigh, feeling my weight;
The balloon releases,
My love spilling out and over
Your flower's fleshy feel.

A Roof for the Rain

All I ask is
A roof for the rain,
An end to this pain,
And for you again;

For you once again.

I am not feeling high;
Keep screaming at the sky
Keeping asking no one "why?"

You are gone.

The pain cuts so deep,
The hurt you cannot know;
With every thought of you,
My heart bleeds;

Torn in two.

Some nights I could die,
Sometimes I almost do;
There is no answer "why?"

I can't be with you.

On A Scarlet Light In Brandon

Why is that light there?
That bloody, red light
That glows scarlet and foggy,
Like Death in the night;
Gazing upon me a constant stare.

What purpose could it meet?
Shining, flowing so thick,
Oozing towards me,
Redder than brick;
Silent sentry out on the street.

How did it come to be?
So tall and glowing so red,
Luminous and bright,
When will it be dead?
Return the colorless night free.

Who put up the light?
Unthinking modern minds,
Uneasy with darkness,
Light, darkness binds;
Light piercing the night.

Where does the light end?
My room or far, far away?
Photons travel unendingly,
Penetrating black and gray;
What meaning does red send?

Growing Up

It appears to me,
At times of great
Discourse;
The very act
Of being kind
Hurts the source.

For, is not by
Doing a favor,
A favor done?
And is not by
Kindness,
Friendship won?

And yet, does not
One often find,
The hurt of sacrifice
Can blur the mind?
As to what purpose
Was the kindness gave;
And turn the giver
To a mindless knave?

Slow Death By Poison

Killing myself,
Doing me in,
Slow death by poison;
Whatever it takes,
As long as I do it
Before I let her
Drive in the stakes.

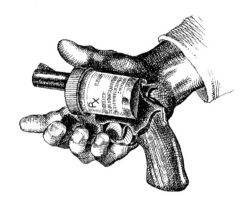

Ride With Me

Oh, won't you ride
With me today,
On a big jet-cloud;

Oh, won't you fly
With me this way,
On such a sunny day;

Michelle?

The clouds are ours,
Quite for our fun;
To laugh and dance,
To sing and run.

Hide-and-seeking
Through flossy fields;
The thrill of love
You truly wield.

Oh, won't you ride
With me today,
On a big jet-cloud;

Oh, won't you fly
With me this way,
On such a sunny day;

Michelle?

Semi-Precious Stones

Think of Life
As a crystal, my friend;
Projecting a myriad
Of points of view.

And everyone who
Has lived and has yet to;
Holds each one of those,
Such that those,
Are each not the same.

Yet, given time,
Two will oppose
Directly;
And, thereby,
Split the crystal.

Cephalic Treasures

Where is the Truth
So cleverly hidden,
That one must spend
A Lifetime to find;
The heavenly knowledge,
Forgotten compassion,
And wordless wisdom
In everyone's mind?

Tears For Challenger

Have you heard?
The shuttle is
Smashed,
Blown up and
Crashed,
Into the waters,
Dashed!

Why, oh why
Do we reach
For the sky?
To blow up is
Worth the try!
Fist of rage,
Tears in eye.

Racing for
The heavens,
Reaching for
God's robe;
Hoping to find,
What is not
On our Globe.

Passing Time With A Rhyme

As puzzling as the questions
Are the answers we receive;
And deception is revealing,
The further we deceive.

Are the visions we are seeing
What we really do perceive?
And are my beliefs something
That I really should believe?

Though I am hiding nothing
And there's "nothing up my sleeve;"
Can you trust the tapestry
That my narrations weave?

If I hide behind honesty,
Am I beyond reprieve;
Even if my purpose
Is not to deceive?

Summer Snow

I like the white, soft pillow
Yet, I weep like a willow
When I picture what it does
To my mind.

But when all hope is lost,
I think of the cost;
And you can't beat the feeling
Of the find.

Wounded Warriors

We are like two
Wounded warriors;
Battered by betrayal,
Lies and pain.

Lovers of life
And seekers of pleasure;
Are we so hurt by life,
That we no longer want
The joys that we treasure?

Some Friend

And so, a friendship dies;
And so, my friend, he lies,
Cheats and steals;
And above all else
Must be suggesting
That I am stupid.

How can he, in
Any form of reality known,
Contrive that I own
Any part of the disputed,
No refuted, debt?

Did he not live
In the comforts of
My warm generosity?
Did he not thrive
Under the shelter
Of my roof, heat and light?

I have, for many nights
Tossed and tumbled
Through my mind
The thought that he might
Possibly be right;

But in no place
In the creations
Of my mind
Can I find
My example
Of his quarrel with me.

A Thousand Lives to Live

If I had a thousand lives to live,
Or a thousand gifts to give;
Not one life, nor one gift,
Would mean as much
As those I'd give to you.

Know this now and ever more
That these few words are true:
You, to me, mean everything
And everything you do,
Fills me with happiness
And truly, I love you.

Jennifer

There's just no way
To get back;
Just no way
To return.

Yet, for forever
Your memory burns,
Etches deep in my mind;
And I've come to find…

That I awake wishing
Only to return,
To the dreams I make
About you and I.

How can I forget
Your eyes and your smile?
Your charm and beauty
To this day beguile.

Can you not see
That you and I
Could forever be
Two parts of one,
Dancing in the sun?

Oh, Jennifer…
I miss you!

Old Man in the Tree

Sitting sullenly
In a tree,
An old man did
Appear to me.

Said not a word,
No voice had he,
Sitting sullenly
In that tree.

Saying something
Without a sound,
He made me start
And turn around.

Hoping no one saw
What I had found,
His saying something
Without a sound.

Hearing truths
Without my ears,
Seemed to cultivate
My fears,
Of seeing blindly
All these years.

Hearing truths
Without my ears.

Questions

To be innocent
Is a virtue,
To be naïve
Is a curse.

Yet, in this
So-called
Modern World;
I wonder,
Which is worse?

For, to say
One is naïve
Is to admit
One does not know;

And innocence
Is ignorance
Of knowledge
Yet to grow.

Nucleo

Up and down,
Round and 'round,
Constantly spinning,
Consciously sinning,
Watch it and see;
Sometimes it hangs,
Spinning, grinning,
Up at something,
Maybe me?

Round and 'round
And 'round again,
I travel through
My mind;
Searching, looking
Everywhere,
For what I
Cannot find.

I struggle, stumble
And trod along,
Cursing every step;
There are even times,
I must confess,
I've sat alone
And wept.

Am I one who,
Among many
It grieves me
To say;
To which all,
Or an infinite amount,
Of Hope is lost?

Wasted Mentality

Suppose I said
That I've been
Inside my head?
What a scene!

You cannot know
Of my despair;
The damage wrought
Beyond repair.

Seedling thoughts
Refuse to sprout,
Beneath the clouds
Of gloom and doubt.

And darker clouds,
One could not know;
Dingy, pitch-black,
Forbid Hope's glow.

Under a dim light,
Deep in my head,
I silently sat
As my soul bled.

Under that light,
I turned my gaze
Upon the waste
Beneath the haze.

Walking alone,
Head in my hands,
Broken morals
Dead in the sands.

I remember
Days in the past,
Honesty ruled,
Principles cast.

Yet, time and
Lost childhood
Have exchanged
Bad for good.

To think that once
I had parents proud;
Now, those that cared
Must laugh aloud.

She Sees Me

I am defined by
The view in her eyes,
Penetrating
And un-holy wise.

I am as she sees me,
Described by her stare;
I bask in the brilliance
Of her glittering glare.

As big as a vision,
As small as a glance;
My limits are outlined
By dreams and chance.

I never feel better,
Nor better perceived;
Than when in her mind,
I am conceived.

I can never contrive,
Nor struggle to be;
All that she thinks
Possible of me.

I can only attempt
To contrive to be,
All that initially
Attracted her to me.

And hope that by Luck,
Destiny or Fate;
I'll become what she
Needs most in a mate.

First Snow

I woke up in
A different
World today,
A world of
Gold and glass.

Peeking through
My curtains,
I had to shield
My eyes from the
Dazzling display,
That would light
A thousand skies.

Through the course
Of night, it seems,
Nature's played
A trick;
While I slept,
Stuck in dreams,
She labored
All the night.

Frosting, painting
And making ice,
Never a moments rest;
For she who
Decorates the world
Can only give her best.

And truth be told
I am amazed
To see the ground
So white;

The frosted trees
And frozen wonders
Constructed
For my sight.

Looking right and
Looking left and
Looking all around,
I cannot find a blemish
Nor a defect
Within view.

The scene appears
So peaceful,
Untouched by
Human hands;
It gives a hint
Of virtue
To this un-pure,
Dirty land.

I tear myself
From looking,
As painful
As that is;
For I'd rather
Recall the
Perfection
Of the
Untouched scene,
Than watch as
The blind
Destroy it;
Footsteps
Raping the art.

Passion For You

Confusion
In my mind,
Blinds me
From my thoughts;

Passion
In my heart,
Consumes me
Like a pyre;

Hunger
In my gut,
Engulfs me
Like a cancer;

…. And the

Glitter
In your eyes,
Adding fuel
To the fire.

A Child Again

Like playing in a sandbox,
Building towns with Tonka Toys,
Filling buildings with plastic people,
Shoebox houses painted by hand.

Like little-league baseball,
Learning to hit and to catch,
Pretending to be some high-paid hero,
Purple bruises forgotten in victory.

Like summer vacation from school,
A seeming eternity to play,
Running through sprinklers,
Living outrageous lives.

When I am with you,
I am a child once more;
Seeing life through awe-struck eyes
Full of Love, Hope and Promise.

Diamond In The Dirt

Like a breeze in the springtime,
She flies through my thoughts;
Like a wave on the rocks,
She crashes onto my heart;
Like a broad beam of sunshine,
She warms my distraught mind;
Like a diamond in the dirt,
She is the rarest of finds.

Like a drink in the desert,
She relieves my lonely thirst;
Like the rain to a flower,
She drips in my senses;
Like a puppy to a child,
She is playful, warm and kind;
Like a diamond in the dirt,
She is the rarest of finds.

Underway

Alone,
Totally alone;
With many a soul in sight.

Surrounded,
People who know the name;
But nothing of the man inside.

Curious,
I wonder how I can stand it;
Leaving my life behind.

Leaving,
Going to sea with strangers;
I must be out of my mind.

Now

Losing weight,
Without a diet;
For the hunger
Lies in my heart,
Now.

Losing sleep,
Learning to cry;
The confusion
Is in my mind,
Now.

Losing thoughts,
Without a care;
For my thoughts
Are owned by you,
Now.

Loving you
Without a doubt;
The pain and joy
Are very real,
Now.

Voyage To The Heavens

A bottle of bubbles,
An incense stick,
Music in the air,
The mood is thick;

Hearts are pounding,
The lights are low,
Anticipation building,
Our minds aglow;

Draped in lace
And full of desire,
She presents herself,
I am set afire;

Together we fall,
Fueled by Love,
Passion carries us
To the stars and above.

Unplanned Events

Life plods on
Tirelessly,
Monotonously;
Each step
Carefully planned,
Yet carelessly lain.

Time drags by
Constantly,
Clinically;
Each moment
Slowing Life's steps,
Increasing the pain.

Motivation,
Inspiration,
Jubilation,
Sensation,
Gone…
All gone.

Drained by
Frustration,
Hesitation,
Confusions,
Delusions.

Nothing planned
Ever works out
Quite the way
It was planned,
Does it?

Better Than Beethoven

Hush, my friend!
Can you not hear?
The concert begins,
Musicians are near.

Alas, he has gone,
Run from the notes;
Gently, ever softly,
Falling in rhythm.

The tempo changes,
The rain pitter-plops;
Splats and splatters
In thick, heavy drops.

A crescendo builds,
As the wind whips harsh;
Blowing and ripping,
Tearing the marsh.

The Cyprus bending,
The Hydrilla swaying,
The roar of the rain;
Nature is praying.

Higher and faster,
Lower and faster still;
All around does abound,
Such a symphonic sound.

Standing alone in awe,
All my senses thrilled;
Immersed in the music,
Ancient promise fulfilled.

Then suddenly, silence!
As if the plug had
Inadvertently been
Pulled, torn from me.

And the music stopped,
No more notes dropped;
Leaving me with
The ducks and the fish.

…And a wish.

Upon Realizing Something Was Wrong

Her silence is
A rusty razor,
Slashing
At my heart;

Cutting like
A hazy laser,
Tearing
Me apart.

The Harder The Hate

Don't know where to go,
Don't know what to know,
Don't like what you have
To show me about myself.

I'm like a gambler,
Down on his luck,
Mad at the world
And I don't give a ____ .

Burning and building,
Churning and growing,
Welling up inside;
If I let it break free,
You'd better run and hide.

The deeper the Love,
The harder the Hate,
I am not responsible
For you or your Fate.

The Love that you gave,
The Hate you now inspire;
Both like a church
With two terrible spires.

Star Thief

How does she do it,
I wonder at night;
How does she rob the
Stars of their light?

I can only conclude
A thief she must be,
To capture their twinkle
With such effortless glee.

Does she woo them?
Or charm them?
Or flash them
Her smile?

And dazzle them
With the brilliance
That was theirs
All the while?

How does she do it,
I wonder at night;
How does she rob the
Stars of their light?

I can only imagine
The things that she's done;
The battles she's fought,
The victories won.

Pink Champagne

She is pink champagne,
All bubbles and fun;
And she glows as warm
And bright as the sun.

Her gossamer hair,
Like softest silk;
Her skin, so creamy,
Like a mother's milk.

With effortless ease,
She lightens the room;
Her smallest of smiles,
Erases my gloom.

Her beauty is pure,
Like new-fallen snow;
That sparkles with hints
Of heaven below.

She is pink champagne,
All bubbles and fun;
And she glows as warm
And bright as the sun.

Getting There

Twelve is a dozen,
Unless you're a baker;
And rules are rules,
But not for lawmakers.

And whether or not
I talk to the sky,
Will the next five years
Not surely pass by?

And if to an end,
This world is to come;
Will not the future
Be important to some?

See Saw

Perched upon a ledge,
I saw;
Near a nearby hedge,
I saw;
Something unbelievable.

Looking at the sky,
I saw;
With unbelieving eye,
I saw;
Something inconceivable.

High above the plain,
I saw;
Indifferent to the pain,
I saw;
Something sensational.

Nature in her glory,
I saw;
Was painting a story,
I saw;
Quite inspirational!

Smothered in purples,
Pinks and blues,
With no color nor shape
Coming in two's;
I shared it with the girl
It reminded me of,
And shivered with the chill
Of the night air above.

Looking in my heart,
I saw;
Turning with a start,
I saw;
A wonderful sight.

Something taking form,
I saw;
Glowing rather warm,
I saw;
An uncommon light.

Amidst the rubble,
I saw;
Despite the trouble,
I saw;
A transformation.

A dazzling sight,
I saw;
Piercing the night,
I saw;
A new creation!

Smothered in purples,
Pinks and blues,
With no color nor shape
Coming in two's;
Dancing with lights
That played in the night,
I shivered despite
The warmth of the sight.

Losing It

My breathing comes
Ragged,
In short, raspy
Gasps.

My throat tastes
Barren,
A wasteland of
Drought.

My skin feels
Chilly,
With a slight sheen of
Sweat.

My hands are
Flexing,
With minds of their
Own.

It's For The Kids

I went for a walk,
Just the other day;
What did I see?
I saw some kids
Trying to play;
But their parents
Kept getting in the way.

Why must we accent
The negative?
Why can't we accept
The positive?
Why can't we just
Do what's right?

I could tell,
Just by their faces,
They were all
Different races;
And came from
Different places;
And just wanted to play.

Why must we enforce
The negative?
Why can't we afford
The positive?
Why can't we just
Do what's right?

Right now, I want
To know why
We plant the
Seeds we grow;
And why, when
It's time to sow,
Do we pretend
We did not know?

Why do we pass on
The negative?
Why do we pass up
The positive?
Why can't we just
Do what's right?

Love Was My Drug

Love was my
Drug of choice;
Yet, many do
As I did.

It spoke in
A strange voice;
Spoke to me
Of you.

Love was my
Drug of choice;
And filled me
With joy.

She Is

She is,
I am sure,
The last of her kind.

She is,
Of course,
Love redefined.

Like seeing
A rainbow
On a rainless day;

Like watching
Some children,
Happy at play;

Like expecting
The rain and
Seeing the sun;

Like catching
Snowflakes
On a laughing tongue;

Like watching
A sunset,
Down in the Keys;

Like finding
A fountain
Of fantasies.

So In Love It's Scary

Although,
Sometimes,
I find
It hard,
To share
Myself
With you;
It does
Not mean
That I
Don't care,
It means
Simply
That I
Am scared.

Reflections

I like the pleasure
Of her by my side,
I like the feel
Of her touch;
I like the pressure
Of her lips on mine,
The kisses I
Cherish so much.

I like the beating
Of her heart with mine,
I like the gleam
In her eye;
I like the breathing
Of her breath so fine,
Her perfume when
She's nearby.

I like that maybe
One day I'll find,
I'll have her for my own;
I like to dream
Of the Love I'll feel,
Knowing how it's
Already grown.

Cobwebs

As dawn draws near,
The day does break;
And I arise,
As I awake.

I clear my throat,
With thirst to slake;
And rattle my head,
Those cobwebs to shake.

Memory hits and
I start to shake;
As reality
Drives in the stake.

Remembering now
My fatal mistake;
The memory starts
My heart to ache.

River of Blood

The river of blood,
From my broken heart;
Threatens to drown me,
Tear me apart.

The river of booze,
That floods my brain;
Comes to the rescue,
Like a runaway train.

Drinking and driving,
Driving you from my brain;
Drinking and driving,
Numbing me from the pain.

The wounds you caused,
Cut me quick and deep;
The wounds forever,
My heart will keep.

The scars might heal
But never fade;
As my soul slips deeper
Into the shade.

Drinking and driving,
Driving you from my brain;
Drinking and driving,
Numbing me from the pain.

Nature's Magic

As my shoes crunch
Along the pine needle rug
That covers the forest floor;
My mind begins to wander,
Mocking my body.

As my legs carry me on
The haphazard journey
That is my morning stroll,
Through trees and ferns and
Plants I'll never know by name;
My mind, unlike the rest of me,
Finds a destination and focus.

She is more beautiful
Than I can describe with words;
The picture that forms in my
Brain is clear and unmoving;
Unlike my eyes which dart about
Constantly,
Ever searching for new and
More colorful sights to see.

As I plod and stumble down
Nature's foyer and wander through
The only church I've ever truly
Known; my brain is thousands
Of miles away, watching me
Dance and play with my
Sweetheart, as if I was seeing
Myself through God's eyes.

Her picture, at first stationary,
Has slowly sped up and is now
Playing through my mind, reliving
Experience after experience;
Showing me over and over the joy
I already know, like a documentary
Without the voices; the scenes
Shift from memory to memory.

Stop – Pause – Play…
Over and over, going through
My mind in a frantic search for
More material; like a crazy-man
In some vast video library
Who cannot see enough of his
Compulsive obsession.

My heart is light and my very
Essence is aglow with true, un-coaxed
Happiness – the kind that makes
You smile and stare for some time;
Until something or someone breaks
The spell, slamming your awareness
Back into reality like a brick through
A window.

I truly enjoy my carefree walks
In the woods; they both inspire
And spark desire; relax me
And make me well again.
Morning service is over, the
Sermon is done and my time,
Once again, has come to an end.

Megan

She is the only child
I will ever have
And she's dead;
Like my friends,
Like my ancestors,
Like my brother.

She is the only child
I will ever have,
With the only woman
I thought I loved;
And she's dead,
Like my brother.

Lady in Black

Death
Looks down
Upon me;
Gazing,
With a
Knowing smile;
Watching
Me work
And toil;
Knowing
I'll be hers
In awhile.

Pleasure and Pain

Pleasure and pain,
Driving me insane,
Rotting my mind;
The two intertwined,
Like Mercury's wand,
The snakes he's so fond of.

Pleasure and pain,
Is its own Novocain;
Deadens in defense,
Then becomes more intense;
Like a storm and its eye,
Like each time I cry.

Liquor of Life

There are times that
Cause my soul to bleed
With the thick, sticky
Liquor of life.

There are times that
Make my mind to think
With the foggy, groggy
Breath of belief.

There are times that
In themselves cause wounds;
Raw and gaping, escaping
Death by living.

There are times that
Test my convictions;
With the fiction of
Conviction by Law.

There are times that
Stretch my desires
To limits and strained
Beyond their means.

There are times that
Stand my hair on end,
Dancing…

Glimpses Through The Window

I sit here…
In a combination of mock-sadness
And anxiety…
Who knows? Not even I…
The extent of my dilemma…
Or even if that is indeed my fate;
Problems, not the one's I should
Think about, plague me…
Distract me.

Ambitions, not goals…
Tear away at my concentration;
My mind, a whirlpool…
My body, sadly out of balance…
My perception, too evolved
To be useful…but my heart beats;
And pumps warmth into my soul…
Inspired by my love…my trust…
Warmed by memories
And remembrances.

My fantasies…
My thoughts surround us
Constantly in scenarios…
Unyielding to the normal
Business of the day;
Smiling, I embrace them…
Holding them as truths.

Their sincerity, not their purity…
Proving them right;
Glittering eyes…
Musical breaths…
Infectious giggles…
The art and music…
Songs in my heart…
Driving its beat;
Pushing it…
Hot, red and warm…
Pulsing life through me,
Pounding passion into me.

Thoroughly…
Completely…
Refreshingly refreshing me…
Arousing me, driving me…
Love and comfort…
Warmth and passion…
Desire and motivation…
All a part of it…
All apart of it…
Loving…
Languishing…
You.

Future Shock

What are we going to tell our children?
What are we going to tell our kids?
What should we tell our sons and daughters
About the things we did?

Should we tell them it was not our fault?
Should we tell them we really tried?
Do we have to tell them anything?
Or do we tell them nothing but lies?

Do we tell them about 9-1-1
And the horror of the dead?
Do we tell them about Iraq,
The invasion so mis-led?

Do we mention Afghanistan,
Our slow descent into Hell?
Do we speak of Armageddon,
The plan we followed so well?

Oh, what do we tell our children?
And what do we tell our kids?
What do we tell our sons and daughters
About the things we did?

Should we tell them it was not our fault?
Should we tell them we really tried?
Should we just do what our parents did,
Every time they lied?

20th Century Eulogy

A jaded sadist?
Well, what can I say?
God, not Man,
Is controlling today.

I must adapt
But I cannot change;
I wish I knew sooner
This world was insane.

The Seals are torn,
The torments unleashed;
Yet the world fails,
Unseeing the Beast.

The Truth sits behind
What we see with our eyes,
Hides in omission;
Reality dressed in lies.

I am only human
Yet, even I can see
That this world
Does not have to be.

What Do I Know?

I do not know a lot of things
And yet, there are a few;
I don't know our destiny
But I do know I love you.

I know at times I can be a drain
And others aren't so bad;
I know at times I bring you down
And others I make you glad.

I know that I will never be
As open as you like;
And yet, to me, I also know
With you, I'm open as I might.

And although I think I know
What the future brings;
My dear, I can let you know,
I don't know everything.

My heart is glad you love me so
And I hope I can return;
All the love you give to me
At each and every turn.

My Darlin', My Darlin'

You are my sweet sugar,
You are my warm sunshine;
The moment I saw you,
I knew that you were mine.

You are my inspiration,
You are my very reason;
Of all the stages of my life,
You are my favorite season.

You bring me laughter,
You give me life;
Your meaning to me,
Is much more than "wife."

You fill me with love,
You sprinkle me with fire;
Watching you be yourself,
Fills me with desire.

You dance through life,
You see through my soul;
The very way I see myself,
As part of a greater whole.

You give me meaning,
You start my day;
Helping me to live,
To laugh and to play.

My Partner,
My Lover,
My Soulmate,
My Darling;

We are both shards of the
Same shattered crystal;
Each different facets of the
Same sparkling jewel.

Alone we shine but
Together we dazzle;
Putting back the magic
Of that once beautiful gem.

We are drawn to each other,
Lifetime after lifetime;
Forever drawn together
By each other's radiant fire.

Wonder Lost

Lost...
Wandering,
The corners of my soul.

Wanting...
Wondering,
What the point ever was.

I'm not mensal...
I'm not mental...
I'm not famous...
I'm not unknown...
I'm not constructed...
I'm not self-made...
I just am, I guess.

But just what that is...
Continues to be
A mystery to me.

I know my wine,
Until it leaves me;
I know my mind,
Until I leave it behind.

Past...
Longing,
For a belief to cling to.

Last...
Place,
Seems to be my pace now.

Wonder,
Lust,
Wanderlust...lost again.

Leaving, Ms. Liberty?

Time does not
Heal all wounds;
But bad memory
Heals everything.

Like forgetting
What she looked like,
How her pillow smelled;
Or forgetting what
She sounded like,
Every time she yelled.

The pain does slowly numb;
As the mind grows ever dumb.

My brain is drained,
I've thought so much;
I've tried to write
But it's not enough.

They just won't listen
To rhyme or story;
They just want to push
Their party's glory.

Chat Room 84-48

A study in stupidity,
This chat room is;
With a lack of lucidity
Is how it lives;
Phrases lacking fluidity
Is what it gives;
Values lacking validity,
Minds like sieves.

A marvelous utility,
Communicate;
Provides feats of futility,
To fornicate;
For those lacking humility,
Humiliate;
Viagra is virility,
Lying in state.

It's a virtual vanity,
These chat windows;
An incite-ful insanity
These chats impose;
Electronic calamity,
Monitor glows;
Hidden human humanity
In plastic clothes.

Virtual Vinland of liars,
Children of greed's;
Simply a global grid of wires,
Fulfilling needs;
Electronic pins and pliers,
Digital seeds;
Countless computers mask desires,
Doing the deeds.

Mindless chatter worthlessly writ,
Idle banter lacking in wit;
Shielded shelters silently sit,
Mentally chomping at the bit.

Personalities permeate,
The screen visually vibrates,
Trying hard to elaborate,
Consensually copulate.

Using all of their skills and wiles,
Traveling electronic miles,
Featuring frowns, anger, and guiles;
Hiding behind digital smiles.

Scrolling screens of ludicrous lies,
Documenting digital spies,
Screaming Freedom's dying cries,
Loving Mother's defeated sighs.

Abbreviated two-letter words,
Try to alleviate your GERD,
Try to search with a mis-spelled word,
Try to teach but the Truth is blurred.

Forgiving all the trials it makes,
And for all the spirit it takes;
Insincerity incubates,
Festering fuel infuriates.

The promise will not be fulfilled,
The designers were very skilled,
Liberty lost by unknown guilds,
Freewill foundered by weakness willed.

One day, maybe, the Golden Age;
Someday, lately, without a Sage;
A day, hopefully, with no cage;
Another dream, another page.

Born Dying

We are born dying,
Even before crying,
Death begins at birth;
We die a little each day;
The trick is to get
As much Life as you can
For each day you die.

Asleep…
I have been waiting
For this day;
Knowing…
And not knowing;
We all already
Know the Truth
We just seek to
Subjugate it
At all costs.

So, we die crying,
Even as we're still trying,
Life begins at Death;
We live a little each day;
The trick is to just
Let it happen…
Naturally.

Virtual Absurdity

Redefining old behavior
On the Internet
As something new;
History's askew.

Webster's downfall,
Technology takeover
Of common speech;
Purity's breached.

MP3 is not music
Nor is it a word;
HTML is not language,
The idea is absurd.

Simple society ,
Reflected in the 'Net,
There really is
Nothing new;
And we have not
Seen it there yet.

Realizing virtuality
Evades actuality,
Subjugates reality,
Inspires surreality.

Ode To The Internet

I've seen it folks, from the start;
Like a child, full of heart;
Fully accessible and free of speech;
I knew it when it was within reach;
Before the companies took it over;
Before the freedoms were taken over;
Back in time, information was free;
No one private or legal tracking me;
No members or passwords or payments;
Anonymous accesses were our raiment's.

Forever Never Ends

I am a knight, not a king;
I am Lancelot
Searching for Arthur;
I can love and kill,
I can create life;
But not without a partner.

I am a ship on the sand,
Pollution in air,
Rain on the ocean;
Who's right after all?
Mitigated Gaul?
Now, that *is* quite a notion!

On a quest without a Grail,
Travel without time,
Path without pleasure;
Consuming with greed,
When nothing is left,
I wonder what is treasure?

Just questions without answers,
I sigh aloud and
Stare at the ceiling;
I ponder the truth
And wonder how God
Can know what I am feeling.

Surely that is the purpose,
He can imagine
It so severely;
She can wonder too,
But how can a God
Know a human sincerely?

Tick tock of the cosmic clock,
Echoing through time,
Minds catatonic;
The immortal lives
Can't know the death toll,
Efficient and atomic.

God reflected in mortals,
Rats running mazes,
Like sand through a sieve;
Strobe-light lives flashing
Miles per minute,
That's how omniscient Gods live.

When I ponder it over,
I really insist,
I can't imagine;
The fate of a god,
To a worthless clod,
Is far too much to fathom.

I just keep walking…
Alone, lone, long, gone.

Man of Steel

If I were a
Man of steel,
It would not
Matter much;
Since I would
Melt anyway,
Beneath your
Loving touch.

If I were a
Chocolate-man,
I'd be a puddle
On the floor;
Dark and sweet,
A sticky blob
Lying by the door.

I could be made
Of diamond;
Or a finely
Chiseled stone;
And still I'd crumble
Into dust,
Whenever
We're alone.

Beautiful Angel

She was taken from Heaven's
Cloudy castle…
She was thrown down to Earth's
Hard, rocky soil…
Taken from Paradise,
She has been tasked to toil.

She has struggled hard
All of her life…
She has been a daughter,
A mother and a wife…
She has lived and loved,
And survived with style.

I did not know her,
Had no idea who she was;
Then, one strange day,
She found me…
Now my eyes are open,
As well as my heart.

She is my beautiful angel,
Sent from Heaven to love me;
She nurtures and protects me,
Loves and excites me,
Inspires and incites me,
Thrills and invites me.

She gives my life meaning,
Gives my freedom direction;
She teaches me without trying;
She lives in my life and I in hers;
We are, in every sense, together…
And I am so lucky!

Rage

I was angry and
Outshined;
And in my madness
I did find,
My darker self
Become refined;
My very soul
Was re-defined;
Until I felt
Myself confined;
And self-control
Was re-assigned;
Hidden hatred
Seized my mind,
As welled-up
Rage
I did unbind.

Are You Receiving Me?

If you are
Reading this,
Am I reaching
You?
Am I getting
To your head?

Are you receiving
Me at all,
Through the cold,
Slick stones that
You used to
Build your wall?

Am I coming
Through at all
My friend,
Or is your
Brain
An empty set?

Am I making
Any sense to you
Or am I wasting
Time,
Trying to introduce
Humanity
To your God-struck
Mind?